D1556238

Books can be purchased at:
www.ashaybythebay.com
www.haywardbookshop.com
www.createspace.com/ 3731508
www.amazon.com
The Book Shop Store, 1007 "B" Street Hayward, CA 94545
(510) 538-3943

ISBN: 1468089471
ISBN 13: 9781468089479

THE CODE SWITCH

Authored by
Ramona L Thomas
Yvetta Doll Franklin

Illustrations by
Tammy Artis

Introduction by Ramona

"The Melting Pot," A metaphor for moving from a heterogeneous society to one that is homogenous. The theory implies that we melt and become one. Our former customs and cultures are left behind and forgotten. This theory promotes devaluing differences. Today Americans are more tolerant of individuality. We're learning to embrace diversity.

The expectation of homogenous articulation of American Standard English is often deemed critical to success. One of our biggest problems concerning language, is the over use of slang in the media. From T.V. commercials to popular music and the Internet, we are bombarded daily with a barrage of slang terminology. It's tightly woven into the fabric of our daily communication.

When slang is introduced, it gains momentum like a snowball. Gradually entering mainstream and ultimately finding its way into America's corporate offices and upper middle-class households. Some slang morphs into acceptable Standard English, becoming the spice and seasoning that adds flavor to our communication. From inception, slang is easily embraced within its birthplace. Unfortunately it's often ridiculed as unintelligent by those outside the founding territory. As slang gains popularity, it reaches beyond its initial borders and eventually is granted admission into more affluent communities. By this time the creators of the flavorful vernacular are not acknowledged.

If you've ever made a mistake and said, "My bad" as opposed to "my mistake", greeted someone by asking "what's happening?" as opposed to "how are you?" or asked the question did you get the "gig"?, as opposed to, did you get the "job"?, or said "bling" to refer to jewelry, you have spoken slang.

The aforementioned describes how slang is an integral part of communication. However, it is important to determine when slang is appropriate to use. "You feel me?" For those non-users of slang, I'm asking, "Do you understand my point?

"The Code Switch" was written to reach out to our youth in hopes making a positive impact on their lives. My prayer is that this work helps to alleviate aggravation for children and adults who are ridiculed for stepping outside their boundaries when choosing to speak Standard English. By the same token, I pray that those who are quick to judge and criticize others for speaking slang are stimulated to take a different view and develop respect language differences.

Let's celebrate those creative minds that freely contribute to American communication, by adding new meaning to words, creating slang which is forever evolving.

Introduction by Yvetta "Doll"

Ramona and I view language out of two different lenses. Ramona is the business-professional career woman. I am the devoted elementary school teacher. Ramona's position in life DOES NOT make her any less educated, articulate or caring. My deportment DOESN'T make me any less professional, business savvy or career minded. So it is with the two main characters in our story. One girl speaks slang, the other articulates Standard English. However, both girls are academic scholars.

When Ramona asked me to collaborate with her about "code switching" I was thrilled, humbled and honored because I want to move kids away from the notion of "fit in where you can get in" to realizing the importance of self worth and good use of language. As an educator I know that children who live in more affluent areas as compared to what is often tagged "The hood" will hear more than 20 million more words than the neighborhood kids.

This reality is sobering! Due to lack of complex language and hefty vocabularies for whatever reasons our children are often overlooked and considered less intellectual. I also feel there is public opinion that the less practice of Standard English and more use of slang depict laziness. Not so! Read this book.

Therefore it is vitally important that "lacking" kids catch up. So, how do we catch up? We have to immerse our children in conversational threads that are educational, global, historical, hypothetical, theological, and scientific and the list goes on. In addition, our kids MUST read. We as parents, adults, aunts, uncles, grandparents, mentors, church members, next door neighbors, etc. must heed the call. Let us embrace, teach, live out, demonstrate, model and encourage effective spoken communication (Standard English) in love.

Ramona and I strongly feel a person should talk the way he or she wishes. Speaking what is comfortable for them. As the old familiar song says: "Express yourself"....However, she and I both know and have experienced the importance of code switching as professionals in the corporate world and interacting with family and friends in casual settings. Just like hitting a light switch to turn lights on or off, so it is with code switching. "There is a time for everything and to everything there is a season."

I receive thirty-two second graders every new school year into my classroom. They are all remarkably precious, wide eyed, excited, energetic and happy little people. I view them as newly built cisterns waiting to be filled..... From their external appearances I can quickly assess most ethnicities. However, it is not until the children speak am I able to determine their skill level or mastery of Standard English. Many of my young students are what I call miniature scholars, but their inability to master good language skills put them at a disadvantage on state writing exams and other demanding California State Standards English tests.

As a final point, it is essential that our young people learn to code switch. Standard English crosses many cultures and opens doors for opportunities, resources and advancement that might otherwise be missed. "The Code Switch" proposes this notion.

Table of Contents

Nonstandard English/Slang Glossary

Slang	Standard
aint	isn't
aintie	aunt
be the bomb	excellent, exciting
bitin off	copy
bootsy	uncool, boring
bout to be smackin	its going to be fun!
cain't	cannot
cool	agreement
cuz	because
doouugghh	dough
doin	doing
down-wit-it	are you in agreement?
evey	every
_fi_	five
fi-ine	very handsome
fitted	dressed with matching **clothing**
fixin ta	I'm going to
frontin	pretending, putting on fake airs
goain	going
goan	going
gots	have

gurl	girl
hate own me	jealous of me
I feel you	I understand you or empathize
my bad	my mistake
member	remember
naw	no
off the chain	above and beyond
oowwn	its happening
pa-leeze	please
phaever	forever
preciate	appreciate
ri-ight	agreement
schahoot	wow!
sho	sure
sho ya right	sure you are right
shuga	term of endearment such as sweetheart
slow her roll	end it
snap	same the say thing at the same time
sole	sold
summo	some more
swag	style
sumthin	something
ta	to
tamarrow	tomorrow
thank	think
that's whats up	that's important
trippin	not thinking clearly

tryin ta	trying to
wanna	want to
we gots	we have
wont	want
yah	you
y-all	you all
yo	your

CHAPTER ONE

Cookie Doouugghh

It's that time of year again; American Brain Child Public School located in the city by the bay, is having its annual spring fundraiser. Both Lavender and Keisha are eager to see who will get the most sales. The past fall's fundraiser, Lavender sold more Christmas wrapping paper than Keisha. This spring the girls are selling cookie dough.

The girls make their plan of attack: Lavender will take the east side of their neighborhood, and Keisha will take her regular west side route.

Keisha decides to wear spring colors because she believes it will enhance her sales. Choosing a soft pale pink headband to match her blouse and socks, she feels like a winner. Before leaving the house, Keisha takes a final look in the mirror and smiles. Her bouncing pony-tail is perfect!

Just before Keisha knocks on the first door, she tells herself, "I got this; Lavender is not *goan* beat me selling cookie dough this year!"

The doorbell rings. "Who is it?" a voice replies faintly.

"What *yah* say?" Keisha asks in a loud voice.

"Who is it?" the voice shrieks.

"My name is Keisha. Can you *pa-leeze* open the door? I'm selling stuff for my school. I was wondering if you'd buy some."

"What kind of stuff are you selling, sweetheart?" The quiet voice inquires.

"Cookie *doouugghh*"

"What flavors?" the slight, raspy voice mutters.

"Well, I got chocolate chip, peanut butter, and oatmeal."

"I'll take one peanut butter," replies the tiny voice.

"Thanks, that'll be *fi* dollars," Keisha replies quickly.

Clearing her throat, the woman with the squeaky voice says, "Did you say fly collars?"

"No, ma'am," says Keisha.

"What did you say, sweetheart? Will you please speak slowly?" asks the hoarse, quiet voice.

Keisha slightly lifts her right hand and begins to erect one pale pink painted fingernail for every number she counts aloud: "One, twoooo, threeee, fourrrr, fivvvve *dol-lars*, *pa-leeze*."

"Hold on a second while I get your money," the soft voice says.

Opening the door, the buyer hurriedly gives a five-dollar bill to Keisha. Keisha hands over a container of peanut butter cookie dough. Keisha has made her first sale on her first attempt. She is feeling confident and believes she will beat Lavender. Encouraging herself, she blurts out, "Come on, feet, let's hit the street!"

Just across the main thoroughfare in the adjoining neighborhood, Lavender heads out to her first house. She bears in mind what her mother constantly tells her: "When you look your best, people notice you. When you do your best, people admire you. When you act your best, people respect you. Go and be your best, daughter."

Lavender always tries to look her best, even though she struggles with her weight. Lavender is not what you would call overweight, but she is munificently pushing the scales. She wishes her clothes fit her better. However, Lavender knows she is more graceful and articulate than Keisha. Therefore, she feels confident she has the competitive edge.

Lavender checks her posture and fluffs her naturally spirally curls. She courageously walks up concrete steps toward a pale gray screen door. She rings the doorbell.

The voice behind the door inquires, "What can I do for you?"

"Hi, my name is Lavender Gray. I attend American Brain Child School. I am selling cookie dough for my school's fundraiser this year. We have three flavors:

chocolate chip, peanut butter, and oatmeal raisin. They are five dollars each. Can I interest you in buying some?"

"You did such a good job on your presentation, I'll take one of each," says the little old lady behind the screen door.

"I'm delighted—thank you for supporting ABC school," Lavender replies with a full-size smile that reveals her perfectly white straight teeth. As Lavender collects money in exchange for the cookie dough, the woman behind the screen door compliments her. "You have such a beautiful smile. It's a perfect match for your lovely skin." Lavender feels pretty. She appreciates the kind words. She smiles and says, "Thank you."

While Keisha is ringing a doorbell, a young child asks, "Who is it?"

"_Um_, you _wanna_ buy some cookie _doouugghh_ for my school?"

"How much is the cookie dough?" the young child wants to know.

Keisha quickly responds, "_Fi dol-lars_."

"Mom, please, please buy some cookie dough," pleads the young boy.

Hearing the boy begging, Keisha smiles because she knows another sale is coming. Flip-flop, flip-flop sounds rush to the white-framed security door. A woman's voice says, "I'll take one container."

"Well, what kind you _wont_," Keisha asks.

"Well, what kind do you have, young lady?" the woman retorts.

"We got chocolate chip, peanut butter, and oatmeal raisin."

"Give me one chocolate chip for my little "*mijo*."

Several thank-yous ring out among Keisha, the woman, and the little boy. Keisha is smiling all the way to her next house, believing, "I'm _goan_ beat Lav for _sho_ this time!"

Meanwhile Lavender approaches a brightly colored blue house on the corner of Diction and Expression streets. She sees a woman on her knees in the yard. She is wearing yellow speckled gardening gloves and an old straw hat. Lavender approaches her and says,

"Hi, my name is Lavender."

"How can I help you, Lavender? I'm very busy. Make it snappy," the woman says as she digs little holes with a handheld shovel.

"Yes, ma'am. I'm selling cookie dough for my school's fundraiser."

"Let's see what kind you're selling," says the tall lady as she extends herself from the ground.

Lavender stretches her neck and nervously responds, "We have chocolate chip, peanut butter, and raisin oatmeal… I mean oatmeal raisin, for five dollars each."

The lady inquires, "How can cookie dough benefit a school, Lavender?"

Lavender collects her nerves and calmly responds, "This money will help our school purchase seedlings, compost bins, water hoses, and planter boxes for our new fruit and vegetable garden."

"In that case, I'll take one chocolate chip and one oatmeal raisin."

Lavender and the lady quickly make their exchange. As Lavender turns to walk away, the lady kindly says, "I'd be willing to donate some of my prize tomato plants for your school's planter boxes."

Lavender smiles with excitement. "Wow! That would be great. Our school is also starting nutrition classes. We will taste lots of veggies and fruits; maybe your tomatoes!" Lavender comments as she walks past sparkling white and red rocks that neatly surround a well-manicured lawn.

Both Lavender and the lady utter quick good-byes.

Knock, knock. Keisha's knuckles rap on the door.

"This me—Keisha, Mrs. Bell," she announces as she sashays through the front door.

"What you want, baby? Duck is at the library." With a confused look on her face, Mrs. Bell asks, "Is this Duck's tutoring day?"

"_Naw_. Um, I'm selling cookie _doouugghh_ for the school. I'm hoping you _goan_ buy some," Keisha urges.

"How much is it, Keisha?" Mrs. Bell asks.

Sounding as if she is begging, Keisha states, "It's only _fi dol-lars_ a container."

"OK, Keisha, I'll buy two."

"But what kind you _wont,_ Mrs. Bell?"

"Well, what kind you got there?" Mrs. Bell comes back with.

Keisha, tilting her head, says, "Chocolate chip, peanut butter, and oatmeal raisin."

So with a slow, deep sigh, Mrs. Bell looks at the numerous containers of cookie dough and says, "Girl, give me one of each, and tell _yo_ mama I'll see her tonight at our line dance class."As Keisha reaches for the containers, Mrs. Bell says, "Girl, you look like the picture of spring."

Keisha's voice rings out, "Thanks. You know I always try to match. See my nails?" she says as she stretches out her slender hands.

Mrs. Bell chuckles and then quickly reminds Keisha, "Your parents work very hard to keep you looking as nice as you do."

"_Sho_ you right. I do love and _preciate_ my folks," Keisha responds.

Mrs. Bell hugs Keisha and tells her, "I'm glad to hear you say you **appreciate** your parents."

"OK." That's fifteen green ones. Thank you, Mrs. Bell. Oops, tell Duck I'll check him out _tamorrow_ at our usual time," Keisha says rapidly as she heads out the door.

"I'm so cool! I rule with the sales this year," Keisha thinks to herself as her contagious smile illuminates her beautiful, smooth Hershey's chocolate skin.

Lavender finally arrives at Old Man Winters' house, as she does every year. She finds him sitting on his front porch reading the obituaries.

"Hi, Mr. Winters," Lavender gleefully greets him.

"Hey, _shuga,_ how _yah doin'_ on this warm spring day?"

"Oh, I'm fine Mr. Winters, and you?"

"I'm blessed, he replies.

What can I do for _yah_?" Mr. Winters asks. His face lights up with a warm grin. Lavender notices the fine gentle creases framing the big smile on Mr. Winters's face.

"It's that time of year again; I'm selling cookie dough for the school's fundraiser. We have chocolate chip, peanut butter, and a delectable oatmeal raisin. They are five dollars each."

"Are you still _doin'_ good in school?" Mr. Winters inquires.

"Yes sir. I earned five A's and one B+."

"Well, that deserves a double order, give me two of each."

Mr. Winters reaches into his pocket and pulls out his old, worn, cracked brown leather bill fold. He takes out his money and hands it to her. A twenty-dollar bill is on top of two tens. He doesn't realize an extra ten is stuck. He gives the money to Lavender.

"Wow, Mr. Winters, thanks for supporting ABC school. Here are two peanut butters, two chocolate chips, and two oatmeal raisins. You always give me the biggest orders. Thanks again," she tells Mr. Winters.

As she turns to walk away, she notices that Mr. Winters has given her forty dollars instead of thirty.

She does an about-face quicker than an eyewink. "Mr. Winters, you gave me too much money." She returns his ten-dollar bill.

He smiles warmly and thinks to himself, "She is a father's dream."

It was twelve years ago, that Mr. Winters lost his wife and daughter in a fatal car crash. Lavender is about the age his daughter would be had she lived. Even Lavender's complexion, the color of the inside of a Reese's Peanut Butter Cup, almost matches his daughter's exactly. Mr. Winters is thankful that he can support Lavender every year. He thinks to himself, "She is so much like my little butter cup."

Both Keisha and Lavender continue knocking on doors and ringing doorbells while attempting to make sales for another half hour. Even though some knocks are unanswered, Lavender continues her course. Her dad always says, "It's not how you start a project but how you finish it." Keisha finishes sooner and gets to the library— their meeting spot—first. As Lavender approaches, she sees Keisha glaring and pointing at her watch. Keisha shouts to Lavender, "_Gurl_, you took _pha-ever_!"

"You need to be more patient, I didn't take **forever**. My last buying customer was Mr. Winters, and I was not going to rush. He's so sweet. He reminds me of my uncle," Lavender expresses.

"No sweat, I feel you," Keisha says as they both smile sincerely at the thought of Mr. Winters.

"Whew, I'm glad we're finished. My feet hurt!" Lavender complains of swollen feet.

"*Gurl*, this fundraising is like *goain* to work, *ain't* it?" says Keisha, as if she knows the demands of a full-time job in the sixth grade.

"It sure is," replies Lavender. The girls laugh wearily while leaning on each other's shoulder.

Keisha believes she has the most sales. She confidently says, "Ooh, *gurl*, I did good this time. I'm so cool."

"You did? How many sales did you make?" Lavender asks.

Keisha brags with one hand on her hip and the other mimicking doors opening, "*Evey* door that got opened, I *sole sumthin*."

Lavender congratulates her. "Wow, good for you!" she says as she knocks knuckles with Keisha, giving the pound.

Keisha asks, "How you do, Lav?"

"Well, I **sold something** to almost every person too. I got turned down at the Wilsons, and three houses didn't even answer."

"Really?" Keisha asks, overly confident.

"Truly," says Lavender with a bit of dismay.

"Well, I *sole* twenty-five dollars' worth," Keisha exclaims with a twinkle in her eye.

Lavender tells Keisha, "That's good. I **sold** fifty-five dollars worth."

Kcisha thinks to herself, OMG (oh my god), she beats me again. Wearing a poker face, she gives Lavender her props, saying, "Go *gurl*." Keisha attempts to look as if she is not shocked, when all the while she is flabbergasted that Lavender beats her once more!

While walking to school the next day, Keisha notices that Lavender has a little bit more pep in her step. "What's up? Why you walking so fast this morning?"

Through the huffs and puffs, Lavender explains,

"I want to see if I have the most sales again. I'm anxious to turn in my cookie dough orders. My mother sold one hundred and ten _dol-lars_ worth at her job."

"Mmm, my dad sold one hundred dollars worth," Keisha states with discontent. With a look of curiosity on her face, Keisha earnestly asks Lavender, "What do you say to get so many orders?"

Lavender stops. "First, I introduce myself. Next, I tell the people what I am selling. Lastly, I give them the price and wait politely for an order."

As the girls continue walking, with a smirk on her face, Keisha says, "Huh, I do the same _thang_."

Lavender thinks to herself, "I know you Keisha, and you do not do the same **thing**."

CHAPTER TWO

The Competition

In the cafeteria, Keisha runs up to Lavender saying, "Ooh, _gurl_, guess what? Today Mrs. Franklin put my name in for student council president. I'm too cool!"

"You won't believe this but the class nominated me for secretary, Lavender says. We may be working together on the student council."

With excitement, Keisha says, "Really?"

Lavender gives her normal response. "Truly."

Moving down the lunch line, the girls enthusiastically yak, yak, and yak about the student council. Keisha whispers, "_Gurl_, I'm _goan_ be running against Julietta Valdez and Keith Kingston. You know, all the girls like Keith because he is _fi-ine_! But between you and me, I _thank_ my real competition is Julietta.

She's tall for her age. She wears a size three dress. Her long light brown hair is always in place. And those large brown almond shaped eyes will hypnotize you." Taking a deep breath Keisha goes on to say, "My *aintie* Tillie says people with big eyes are honest. Julietta speaks three languages: Spanish, English, and Tagalog. She is funny, always cracking jokes, and wants to be a pilot for the air force."

Lavender assures Keisha, "I really **think** you have this in the bag."

"Do you really *thank* so, Lav?" Keisha asks nervously.

"Truly, Ke Ke," responds Lavender.

With that being said, Keisha turns to Lavender and says, "You so lucky, you don't have *no* competition for the secretary job."

Feeling insulted, Lavender turns her lip up and quickly says, "You're right! I don't have **any** competition, but I'm the best person for the job."

Keisha realizes, Lavender is right, so she shrewdly says, "Since you don't have any competition, I know you *goan* help your best friend win."

She smiles. Looking directly at Keisha, Lavender responds, "Of course, I am **going** to help you win!"

Keisha sighs with relief, responding, "Cool!"

For the past week, Julietta, Keith, and Keisha have campaigned intensely. Each candidate gave a two-minute speech over the school's intercom system. The contenders had a blurb in the school newspaper. Colorful posters promoting the candidates were placed all around the school campus. The competition was fierce.

While walking to school, Keisha appears antsy. She shouts out, "Lav, I *cain't* wait till *tamorrow.*"

"You **can't**? Why?" Lavender asks.

"Don't you *member*? It's *votin* day *tamorrow*. I hope I'm *goan* win and be president."

"Yes, I **remember** we are **voting**, and you are **going** to win **tomorrow**!" Lavender declares with a wide smile, showing off her pearly whites.

Keisha doubts herself again by asking, "Really, really?"

Lavender reassures her, "Truly, truly!" Lavender knows hard work pays off. She won the school's spelling bee two years ago. Lavender set aside one hour every day to review her words. This commitment often meant missing choir practice and bike riding. Sometimes, hanging out at the mall shopping, eating in the food court, and playing video games in the arcade was a no-no. She learned one has to deep down believe in him or herself. The girls have worked hard promoting Keisha for president.

Lavender reminds Keisha, "Do not forget all the work that's been done. First we made the largest and most colorful posters. Next, we gave out chocolate kisses at the end of class last Friday. Our lunch crew made ribbons with your initials on them. Your name is all over the computer lab. And don't forget Mrs. Franklin, the school counselor put your name in the hat! All the kids respect Mrs. Franklin."

Keisha responds, "*Sho ya* right, *gurl*. I was *trippin* for a minute."

Lavender assures her, "**Sure I'm** right. You will see when the votes are counted tomorrow."

"See you at recess," fills the air as the girls separate for their classes.

CHAPTER THREE

Summo Votes

Finally… Friday arrives.

"My, my, look who's walking fast today," Lavender points out as she nearly trips trying to keep up with Keisha's fast pace.

"_Gurl_, I _wont summo_ votes. I'm trying to hurry up so I can ask for _mo_ votes before school starts."

"I'm proud that you are trying to get **some more** votes. You're acting like a real politician, campaigning to the end," says Lavender with a raised fist.

The day moves slower than an old turtle on a hot rock. Finally the clock strikes 2:45 p.m. The voice over the intercom interrupts the day. "Please excuse the interruption, teachers and students. May I have your attention?

The student council votes have been counted. We are ready to announce the results.

"Our new treasurer is Wayne Watson in room sixteen; vice treasurer is Stina Fatona from room eight. Our secretary is Lavender Gray in room seven. Assistant secretary is Debrell Johnson in room ten. Our timekeeper is Dante Daniels in portable two. Assistant timekeeper is Stephanie Singh. She is in room six. Before announcing the class president, we want to thank the presidential candidates for such hard work. You three should be very proud of your efforts. Our new class president is none other than the vibrant, talented, all-around math wizard Keishaaa Wilkerson from room eight. Let's all applaud our new student council members." Cheering and applause could be heard over the intercom and throughout the halls.

The three o'clock bell rings. Keisha and Lavender run to meet each other with open arms. Lavender screams with joy, "I told you, Keke, you would win!"

"You _sho_ did," Keisha responds as she jumps up and down in one spot.

"**I sure** did, didn't I?" Lavender chants, "You did it, you did it!" as they jump faster together, holding hands. The girls soon create a rhyme:

"We did it, we did it, we can't quit it."
"We did it, we did it, we must admit it."
"We did it, we did it, oh yeah, we did it!"

Keisha whispers, "_Gurl_, when we get out the building, I'm _goan_ to tell you the first _thang_ I _wanna_ do as president."

Lavender answers, "I can't wait to hear what it is you **want** to do."

After crossing the street, Keisha looks around as though she is a spy. She reveals in a whisper, "_Gurl_, for our first council meeting, I'm _goan_ present my plan for a school dance."

"Why are you whispering? That's not so different," Lavender says.

"My plan is to have a dance with a twist, something really different. It's _goan_ be the bomb!" Keisha explains.

"Well, tell me, what's the twist?" Lavender wants to know.

"The twist is serving healthy snacks and nutritious foods. What do you think Lav?"

Lavender doesn't respond immediately. She is a true fan of junk food. Lavender enjoys eating pizza, hot dogs, cakes, pies, cookies, and candy, all of which is usually sold at school fundraisers. "I guess it's a good idea," she replies hesitantly.

"You don't sound so sure."

"Well, a lot of us like eating junk food. To tell the truth, healthy snacks sound a little boring."

"I guess we'll have to see how the rest of the council feels about it, when we meet on Monday." Keisha says with a smirk.

The girls reach the corner of Diction and Expression. Keisha turns right on Diction and Lavender continues on Expression.

They both twirl and yell to each other.

"Kisses!"

"Smooches!"

"Bye!"

CHAPTER FOUR

The Proposal

The school bell rings at 1:00 p.m. because it is minimum day. The council members are so excited about their first meeting. Keisha and Lavender meet at their usual spot. The girls hold hands as they skip into the cafeteria. The Vice Principal, Mr. Keith Nickens, is seated at the head of the table next to Mr. Elbert Thomas. The council members are wide-eyed.

Mr. Nickens opens the meeting with introductions. "Good afternoon, council. I am your lead adviser; however, the extracurricular school activities will come from this group. To my left is our parent-community liaison, Mr. Elbert Thomas."

Mr. Thomas interjects by raising his hand and says, "You council members may call me Mr. E."

Mr. Nickens continues, explaining "Mr. Thomas is volunteering his assistance with this group. Mr. Thomas or I will attend every student council meeting. Here are our expectations:

1. **B**e on time to all meetings.
2. **L**isten when a fellow member speaks.
3. **R**espect others ideas and opinions.
4. **M**ajority votes will rule."

Looking in the students' faces, Mr. Nickens asks, "Are there any questions?"

"I'm going to turn the meeting over to Keisha, our president." As Keisha looks around the table, Mr. Nickens reassures her holding his thumb up. "Mr. Thomas and I are here to support and guide the group." Keisha can't wait to talk about her idea of the school dance.

"Hey, *y'all*, I got this really neat idea to make money for the school and put us on the map!" While raising her hand, Keisha slowly rubs her thumb across the tips of her fingers, gesturing money. The council quickly gets the idea.

The treasurer, Wayne Watson, raises his hand and asks, "What is your proposal, Keisha?"

Keisha looks deeply at the faces of her council and says, "Let's have a school dance, but let's serve healthy foods!"

Mr. Nickens and Mr. Thomas glance at each other, smiling. Stina Fatona, vice treasurer comments under her breath, "Sounds _bootsy_ to me." The timekeeper, Dante Daniels, raises his hand and asks, "Is pepperoni pizza healthy?" The council members laugh. Mr. Nickens chuckles too. "Yeah," one voice says.

No it's not," says another. The council members immediately look directly at their leaders. Both men point to Keisha and say,"You are the president. This is your cabinet. You guys will discuss, decide, and vote, remember?" With a serious look, Keisha says, "Pizza can be healthy if you eat in moderation. _Y'all_ know calcium helps to build strong bones. That's the cheese. But too much cheese can make _yah_ fat," she concludes as her eyes drift toward Lavender.

Debrell Johnson, Assistant Secretary blurts out, "Make me fat!" Stina and Debrell slap hands with open palms. Mr. Nickens reminds the group, "Remember, follow protocol by raising your hand."

"Oh, _my bad_, I'm sorry," replies Debrell. Keisha recognizes Lavender's hand and gives her the floor.

"Thanks, Ke. Sometimes it's genetics that makes a person thick. So will pizza be offered or not?" Keisha takes the lead and tells the team, "Let's put it to a vote. All in favor for pizza raise your hands."

Four hands shoot straight up in the air like rockets on the Fourth of July. Stephanie Singh, Assistant Timekeeper, who didn't vote for pizza and Keisha are defeated. Keisha goes on and says, "Let me tell _y'all_ the rest of my plan. I _thank_ we will be on point if we replace some of the usual snacks with nutritious choices. We'll be recognized for being leaders in offering healthy choices. Plus, some of our classmates could stand to lose a few pounds." Keisha makes sure she doesn't look in Lavender's direction.

"Let's try air-popped popcorn. How about baked fries and chips? Let's have pretzels instead of regular potato chips and hot munchies. Will _y'all pa-leeze_ consider yogurt-covered raisins and yogurts as a substitute for our usual candy? Let's offer bottled water and sports drinks instead of sodas. My last idea is turkey burgers and chicken hot dogs to add to our new healthy selections." Waiting a moment or two for this all to sink in, Keisha asks, "So are _y'all_ down _wit_ it?"

Stephanie raises her hand and says, "I think this is a great idea! People will have healthy choices now. Don't forget we are supposed to get in our five a day she reminds the group. Ms. Dornacher, our nutrition/garden teacher, says five fruits and vegetables every day make the body strong."

Lavender raises her hand and reminds the council, "But my mom always bakes the tea cakes, and Mrs. Grotto makes delicious brownies." Keisha thinks to herself. "I _sho do_ love Mrs. Gray's tea cakes." Dante raises his hand and says, "I don't want to give up hot spicy munchies, because they are my favorite."

Time is slipping away. Mr. Nickens alerts the council to wrap up the discussion. Keisha stands and quickly says,

"_Okaaay_, all in favor of this menu:
Fruit and vegetable trays
Air-popped popcorn
Pretzels
Bottled water

Yogurt
Yogurt-covered raisins
Low-sugar sports drinks
Pizza
Turkey burgers
Chicken hot dogs
Tea cakes
Pa-leeze raise _y'all_ hands."

A big smile comes across Keisha's face as the proposal passes five to one. Lavender was the lone "no" voter. Mr. E tells the council he will inform parents and the community of the upcoming event. "The parents will be excited to support your healthy-choice menu. Council, I'm very pleased with the handling of your first meeting. All you have to do is decorate the gym, and you have two weeks to get it done. I actually can't wait to see it all come to fruition," Mr. Nickens says.

Lavender responds, "Even though I voted against your proposal Keisha, I still support the team. With our skills and team effort, we can do this!" Snapping her fingers and doing a victory dance, Keisha sings, "It's _oowwn_, it's _oowwn_." Mr. Nickens congratulates the council and says, "Yes, it's **on**!"

CHAPTER FIVE

The Mad Rush

Keisha patiently waits at the girls' usual morning meeting spot, thinking, "Lavender is never late. *Sumthin* must be up."

Grabbing her cell phone, she calls Lavender. "*Gurl, where you at*? Just *cuz* we had a long weekend don't mean we can be late today. We *gots* ten minutes to get to our Tuesday science lab."

Gasping for breath, Lavender says, "No worries, I'm two houses away. **Where are you**? Do you see me?"

Keisha, stretching her neck, says, "Oh, I see you now."

"I overslept, sorry I'm late. I was completing my essay on the etymology of cartoons. Our computer was down for hours."

The girls move with pep in their step. Keisha knows that Lavender's running is more like light jogging. She's a little too heavy to run fast.

They arrive to school two minutes before the bell rings. At recess, Keisha tells Lavender, "The dance is _goan_ be the bomb, Lav."

At lunch with excitement, Keisha whispers to Lav, "The dance _goan_ be off the chain!"

"I hear you! The dance is **going** to be the best American Brain Child School has ever had!" Lavender affirms.

Placing her hand on her narrow hip, Keisha confirms, "I know that's right!"

Keisha continues, Mr. E will manage security, the DJ, and parent chaperones."

CHAPTER SIX

The Dance

The student council members are standing on the right and left side of Keisha. They are anxiously waiting to welcome students to their first organized spring dance. They gaze as the students enter the cafeteria. Some are hopping and bopping. Some are running and looking cunning. Others are gliding and sliding. The shy kids enter incognito.

The VP walks onstage and gives Keisha the microphone. She drops it and then quickly picks it up, attempting to look cool and calm. "_Y'all_ know I did that on purpose." Placing her right hand on her right hip she says, "Y'_all_ go ahead and lol. For those of you who don't know lol means, "Laugh out loud!"

The students are chanting, "Go Keisha, go Keisha, go council, go council!"

Keisha is wearing her favorite outfit that matches the school colors; green and white. Even her hair bow is green and white checkered. She is mesmerized by the attention. A huge smile comes across her face. She beams with joy and excitement; and suddenly she becomes nervous. She begins to shake like a leaf on a tree on a windy autumn day.

Lavender, standing on Keisha's immediate right, nudges her gently and whispers, "You can do this."

Keisha steps forward and begins her speech. "Thank you for coming to our student council's first endeavor. The money raised from this year's school dance will help support our school's enrichment programs. This includes our end-of-the-school-year field trip. Some of you may have already noticed the new food additions. My team and I have made some menu changes. We are offering fresh vegetables, turkey burgers, and chicken hot dogs. The vegetable trays have been donated by parents and school staff. Oh, one more thing, we are offering baked fries too. Instead of candy you can choose flavored yogurts, yogurt-covered raisins or pretzels."

"The restrooms are open for us. The committee and I have worked long and hard putting this wonderful dance together for you." Keisha quickly turns, faces the council with a tear in her eye, and says, "Thank you team!" Facing her audience again, she continues, "Lastly, thank you, parents and teachers, for your contributions and for chaperoning our dance. So now, let's get our party <u>own</u>."

She turns to her council and says, "*<u>It's bout ta be smackin</u>!*" Lavender tugs Keisha's sleeve and whispers, "**Yes our dance is about to become a hit** everyone will have a great time."

The audience explodes with clapping.

CHAPTER SEVEN

The Nomination

While walking to school that Monday after the dance, Lavender compliments Keisha. "You really did a good job leading the student council.

The dance was a huge success! So was the healthy menu!"

Overly confident, Keisha beams, "_Sho you right_, and it was the _bomb_."

Lavender asks, "Did you mean to say **you're** right? Because it seems like you've been _frontin'_. You spoke so well at the dance."

Shocked and insulted, Keisha responds, "What you _tryin ta_ say, Lav?"

"I'm **trying to** say, you've been acting like you can't speak proper English, yet you surprised everybody with your speech at the dance."

Keisha ponders over her best friend's comments as they finish their walk to school.

At recess, Keisha runs up to Lavender to inform her that Mr. Boyd wants to see her at prep, in the math classroom. Keisha cannot hang with Lavender today.

Lavender responds, "It's ok, because the VP wants to see me in his office during prep time too."

As both girls head back to class, they wonder what's up.

Returning to her math classroom for her meeting with Mr. Boyd, Keisha says, "I'm here."

"Great, I'll be with you in a minute. Sit at your desk," he replies.

"Excuse me, Mr. Nickens, you requested to see me." Lavender states while knocking on his office door.

"Oh, thanks for coming. I'll be right with you Lavender; please take a seat," Mr. Nickens offers.

Mr. Boyd positions his seat in front of Keisha. "I was very impressed with your leadership. The student council worked well together, and your speech was inspiring. I've never heard you speak so well."

Keisha gloats and says, "Thanks, Mr. Boyd."

Mr. Boyd looks directly at Keisha. With a serious stare, he says, "I asked you to come today for two reasons as he holds up two fingers. First, I want to congratulate you on scoring the highest percentage on the sixth-grade math cumulative test. It is students like you who make me proud to be a teacher. Secondly, you really surprised me and all the teachers with your speech."

Keisha responds, "You know, Mr. Boyd, my best friend, Lavender, said the same _thang ta_ me this morning on the way to school."

"Do you mean to say she said the same **thing**?" Mr. Boyd questions her. With test scores in one hand and a nomination letter in the other, Mr. Boyd tells Keisha, "I am nominating you for valedictorian."

Keisha can't believe her ears. "Wow me?" She pinches herself to see if she is dreaming. "Thank you, Mr. Boyd! This is really cool!"

With a stern look, Mr. Boyd explains, "Keisha, in order to be a serious valedictorian candidate, you must continue to speak as you did at the dance. You showed us all that you have it in you." He further explains, "There are many opportunities for you, young lady, but you must be able to speak well. You know, Keisha, there is a time and a place for fun language and for Standard English." Keisha pays close attention to Mr. Boyd's every word.

Mr. Boyd asks, "Have you ever heard the term code switching?" Keisha is unaware of what Mr. Boyd is talking about. Trying to act smart, she replies, "Switching is how fast girls walk past cute boys." Mr. Boyd, giving off a hearty laugh, promptly states "That is not the answer I am looking for young lady."

Keisha speculates this must have something to do with math or science, and says, "Code switching must be when you change your mathematical computations to arrive at the original numbers of a problem once you've figured out your answer." Again, Mr. Boyd tells Keisha, "That is not the answer, but I appreciate your persistency."

Keisha bashfully asks, "What is code switching?" Mr. Boyd clears his throat and leans in a little closer and begins. "Code switching is the ability to alternate between one or more languages or dialects." He explains, "There is a time to be formal, as you spoke at the dance." Keisha continues to listen, slightly bobbing her head up and down. "There is a time to be informal, as when discussing your favorite singer with friends. It all has to do with your audience." Mr. Boyd explains that when young people talk slang, they are often viewed as unintelligent and unworthy of advancement. This is a tragedy, but regretfully it is the mind-set of many powerful people who may one day interview you for employment and or college entrance."

He gives examples. "Instead of saying 'Keep it real,' one could say, 'I'm being honest or sincere.' He continues, "Another way of saying I'm cool is to say 'I understand' or 'I'm ok with that.'"Finally, he asks Keisha, "Does this help? I hope you understand what I'm saying to you today, Ms. Valedictorian."

Second-guessing herself, she asks, "Really…me, Mr. Boyd?"

Mr. Boyd reassures her, "Yes, you have what it takes. You just have to let it shine."

As Keisha walks away, she remembers the refrain of an old familiar gospel song, "I'm gonna let it shine, let it shine, let it shine."

In the meantime, Mr. Nickens turns his swivel chair to face Lavender. "Young lady, you have made me and the staff extremely proud. You always step up to the plate, volunteering for student council secretary, helping your classroom teachers, and peer tutoring. You've been on honor roll since third grade. I'm nominating you for valedictorian!"

Lavender responds, "Wow, Mr. Nickens, thank you for believing in me. I am so excited. I am honored. My family is going to be so proud of me!"

The three o'clock bell rings. Lavender can't wait to meet Keisha and tell her the good news. As she waits at their usual spot, Keisha approaches her with an unusual pep in her step. Lavender notices a zest she had not seen before.

As the girls leave school and the crowds dissipate, Keisha reports in a soft voice, "You will never ever guess what happened to me today at prep!"

Lavender says, "Tell me, because I have something big to tell you too."

Keisha says, "Well, tell me, Lav."

Lavender respectfully declines, saying, "No, you go."

Keisha replies, "_Naw_, you always listen to me. What's up, Lav?"

Lavender says, "You go."

Keisha says, "_Naw_, you go."

Lavender then says, "Okay let's both say it on the count of three. One, twooooo, threeeeeee."

They both blurt out simultaneously, "I might be VALEDICTORIAN!!!!"

"Oh, *snap*," Keisha responds. Then there is total silence between the two girls. They stare at each other in astonishment with their mouths wide open. It is as though time is standing still. Cars are moving, people are talking, horns are honking, they hear nothing but "I might be valedictorian," like a broken MP3 player echoing over and over again.

After what seems like forever, the girls finally speak, each saying, "Me too."

Next, Lavender asks Keisha, "Who selected you?"

Keisha quickly asks with a raised voice, "Who picked you, Lav?"

While Lavender is saying "The vice principal," Keisha interrupts and says, "Mr. Boyd picked me."

Reality hits Keisha. She thinks to herself, "Lav talks way better than me." She realizes that she'll be competing against her best friend, who is very articulate. Doubting herself again, she sheepishly asks Lavender, "Do you want it, Lav?"

Lavender hears the awkwardness in Keisha's voice and decides to tell her the truth in her most kind voice. "Yes, I do, Ke. I'm honored. Besides, I've made honor roll the last three years. I feel like I deserve this."

For the first time ever, the girls walk home together in entire silence. As they are walking, Keisha contemplates, "What about me? *I got skills*." She thinks about the things she does well. "I'm good in math. I'm good in science. I'm a good algebra tutor. I'm a good cheerleader. I'm cool. I have _swag,_ and everybody knows _that's what's up_. After all, I am the student council president, and I'm cute too. _Shahoot it's all good_!"

They reach their splitting point. Speaking after all, they awkwardly utter, "Kisses" "Smooches."

Neither girl looks directly at each other.

CHAPTER EIGHT

The Argument

It begins to rain. Lavender shares her small umbrella with Keisha. The red light catches the girls. Lavender turns to Keisha, stating, "Yesterday you asked me if I wanted to be valedictorian. I never asked you. Do you want it, Keke?"

Keisha answers back, "Absolutely I want it. Last night I thought about it and decided that Mr. Boyd is right. I do have what it takes to be valedictorian."

Lavender admits, "I'm surprised he asked you."

"Why you shocked?" Keisha snaps and raises her voice.

Lavender explains, "Well, you don't speak proper English, and the valedictorian gives the graduation speech."

Keisha asks, "What do you mean by proper?"

Lavender responds, "You don't speak normal."

Keisha says, "What's normal Lav? What's normal to you Lav, may not be normal to me. Our crew at ABC thinks you don't speak normal; you're the odd ball."

Lavender takes in such a deep breath, her chest rises. She responds, "Well guess what Keisha; the world is bigger than our crew at ABC."

Keisha rolls her shoulders back. She stands erect and informs Lavender, "I too can speak _good_ English, and that's just what I'll do from now on."

Lavender wants to know, "Why haven't you before now? You could have fooled me."

Keisha scrunches her eyes and nose, thinking no, she didn't. Then she asks Lav, "_Is you tryin ta hate own me?_"

Lavender retorts, "Keisha, you just said that you too can speak **proper** English. So, when do you plan to start?" She leans in close to Keisha's face. What you just said to me was not Standard English. What you should have said is, '**Are you trying to hate on me**?'" Lavender says as her neck protrudes out like a chicken.

Keisha looks at Lavender, rolls her neck, cuts her eyes, turns her shoulders and says," It's time for class." She hurriedly walks away.

For the first time in the girls' seven years of friend-ship, they are at odds with one another.

Keisha and Lavender somehow avoid each other during morning recess.

At lunch, Lavender and the crew are already seated at their table. While Keisha slides her tray getting her food, she notices the group. Looking at Lavender, she thinks, "Should I join them, or should I go to another table?" Before she completes her thought, Julietta motions her over. She joins them and takes her seat next to Lavender, as if everything is normal.

Keisha usually is the last to join the group because she buys the school lunch. Keisha's mom is a head nurse and sometimes has to work double shifts. The other crew members usually bring their meals from home. Wayne notices that Keisha is quieter than normal and asks, "Keisha, are you _bitin off_ Lavender. Why you so quiet today?"

Usually during lunch, Lavender listens more while Keisha leads the conversations.

Keisha responds to Wayne's question with her eyes looking away, and answers, "No."

By this time everyone starts sharing desserts. Lavender knows that Keisha loves her mother's homemade tea cakes. She has extra in her plastic bag. Hesitating, she wonders, "Should I offer Keisha a tea cake or not?" She thinks to herself, I spoke pretty harshly to Keisha this morning." As she ponders, she hears her big mama's voice saying, "If you want a friend, be a friend. This world would be a lot better off if people would forgive and forget." Her hand automatically reaches into her plastic baggy, takes out one tea cake, and gently gives it to Keisha. A smile makes its way across Keisha's face. She warmly says, "Thank you, Lav."

"You're welcome. You know you're still my BFF," (Best Friend Forever) Lavender softly replies. All of a sudden Keisha experiences a robust feeling of how precious her and Lavender's friendship is. She wants to hug Lavender as tight as she can, but she feels embarrassed at the thought.

"Really?" Keisha asks.

"Truly," Lavender responds.

At the end of the day, the girls do their customary walk home. They talk about homework, teachers, the latest fashions, music, and friends.

They reach their departing point. Keisha gives her usual expression, "Kisses," and Lavender responds with "Smooches."

CHAPTER NINE

The Decision

Staff meetings are held on Wednesdays because it's minimum day. Over the intercom, the normal announcement is made. "Staff it is 12:55 pm. Please make your way down to room eleven for the weekly grade-level collaboration."

Teachers enter into a classroom brightly lit by the natural sunlight entering from the rear windows. The walls are covered with posters of language-arts teaching strategies. The left side of the room has colorful buckets of books. The right side of the room has about ten laptops sitting on a rectangular table. The center of the room has six rectangular tables where teachers gather and sit. In the rear corner of the room is a kidney-shaped table that seats five children for small group instruction. There is an old teacher's desk with a black high-back chair.

As the teachers enter the room, they grab their agendas and bottled water from the small table by the door. They each take their seats at their grade-level tables.

The VP, Mr. Nickens, welcomes the teachers by asking, "Are there any ROSE recognitions today?"

Recognition **Of S**pecial **E**ffort.

Mr. Smith, who teaches kindergarten, recognizes Mrs. Hill, one of the Instructional Assistants, with a plastic rose. She assisted him with a science garden project. The kids planted sunflower seeds.

Ms. Wong, a fifth grade teacher, recognize the librarian with a plastic rose for opening the library so students could play antonym/synonym games on the desktop computers during lunch.

The staff applauds the two rose recognitions. Afterward, the VP says, "Let's look at our agenda; we have a lot to cover."

The agenda reads:

1. Report cards are due in three weeks.
2. Student Council
3. Valedictorian Nominations
4. Fundraiser
5. Spelling Bee for grades four, five, and six next month. Each teacher selects ten words from your reading anthologies.
6. Science Fair

Mr. Nickens reminds the staff that report cards are due in three weeks not four.

He also tells them that the student council has planned a spirit day for next Friday. They're calling it Backwards Day. Blouses and shirts can be worn backward, and backpacks will more than likely be worn on children's chests rather than their backs. The teachers laugh.

Mr. Nickens brings up the third item on the agenda. "It's time to consider, nominate, and vote for this year's valedictorian. Some considerations are attendance, grade point average, citizenship, leadership and test scores."

Right away, Mr. Boyd gets the attention of the VP by lifting his water bottle and slightly shaking it. Mr. Boyd is not tall or short, he is in between. Some of the boys in his class are actually taller than him. His large brown eyes are like a perfect ring. They appear oversize because he wears such large eye glasses. The kids have nicknamed him "The Nerdy Professor." He says, "After looking over my student's math test scores, I have a recommendation for valedictorian." He gazes at the expressions of his peers. He is thinking to himself, "I've carried the highest math scores for the past two years throughout the district. I know my colleagues trust me."

Mr. Wilson, a seventh grade teacher, sitting across the table from Mr. Boyd comments, "That's great, but shouldn't we consider all the variables?"

Mr. Boyd directly responds to the statement. "I have considered more than just math scores. This individual has excellent attendance, great citizenship, and exudes leadership. She is our current student council president,

Keisha Wilkerson. She's the highest-scoring math student among all the sixth-graders," he proudly boasts.

The teachers begin chatting. "One states, He has a point." Then another teacher comments, "She's only the student council president because her friends voted her in." A different teacher responds, "But that's the point, and she did get the majority of votes." Mr. Boyd reminds the staff, "We've had the highest math scores in the district since I came on board. I think I've made the best selection out of the whole student body."

Mr. Nickens graciously thanks Mr. Boyd and the staff for their dialogue and asks, "Are there any more nominations?"

"Yes, I have one," Mrs. Sanchez, a tenured teacher, answers from across the room. Her light cream complexion and bleached blond hair emphasizes her red shaded lipstick, finger nails and toenails. Because she wears open toe sandals most all school year, the kids sneak and call her "Miss Glamor." "I'd like to nominate Lavender Gray. She fits the bill."

Mr. Nickens is pleased because he was going to recommend Lavender. It is evident that at least one other staff member notices her qualities.

"Lavender has academic supremacy, and she is a confident student," Mrs. Sanchez says. She has drive; she is ambitious and accepts challenges. Lavender has been a great role model for ABC school, and let us not disregard she's been on honor roll since third grade." She elaborates in such great lengths because she knows Mr. Boyd has also presented a strong candidate.

Mrs. Sanchez continues. "For the past couple of years, Lavender has frequently stopped by the front office to offer her assistance. She photocopies and takes materials to classrooms. She helps the office manager distribute mail in teachers' boxes. In addition, she is a study-buddy for kindergartners and first-graders during their reading block. Lavender is the student council secretary. Not only does she help Keisha, she supports the entire council." When Mrs. Sanchez finishes her explanation in support of Lavender, a pin drop could be heard. All eyes are on Mrs. Sanchez, including Mr. Boyd's.

Mr. Nickens breaks the unusual silence by stating, "We've heard two very strong arguments for valedictorian. Are there any more nominations?

Well, since we only have these two, I'll open the floor for further discussion."

"You know, Keisha's speech was very impressive at the school dance," a teacher says. Ms. Ella, the computer lab assistant interjects, "The whole council, especially Lavender, supported Keisha, she didn't do it alone." Someone blurts out, "That's true. However, teamwork is a good attribute, and Keisha has demonstrated great leadership." Several more teachers chime in their opinions about both girls. Comments are insightful and constructive.

As the meeting is about to end, the principal, Opal Lee Blackwell, enters the room. She is quickly brought up to speed with the ongoing dialogue. She listens intently for several minutes before saying anything. Mrs. Blackwell insists the valedictorian vote be a majority staff decision. She informs the staff, "This is not a top-down decision."

Mr. Boyd gingerly asks, "When do you want our decision?"

"Thanks for asking. I cannot predict the outcome, but I know we will come to a happy medium on this. Let's have our votes in by Friday. That gives us three days," Mrs. Blackwell says with a rather stern look and quick smile.

CHAPTER TEN

Code Switching

The teachers file one by one into the staff lounge for the valedictorian vote. First Mr. Boyd enters but doesn't take his normal seat. Rather he stands and watches as the other teachers enter. Mrs. Sanchez enters confidently and greets Mr. Boyd. She too stands as they wait for other teachers to be seated. Finally Mrs. Blackwell comes in. She begins, "Thank you, staff, for coming to share your voice. We've had three days to think about the best choice for valedictorian. I trust that all of us have given much consideration to our decision.

"The valedictorian is someone whom we have embraced, shaped, and encouraged to be the best she can be. Now I'd like each of you by show of hands to vote for either Keisha Wilkerson or Lavender Gray. All in favor of Mr. Boyd's nominee, our current student council president Keisha Wilkerson, please raise your hand now." Mrs. Blackwell counts the raised hands. "One, two… Thank you.

"All those in favor of Lavender Gray, Mrs. Sanchez's nominee, please raise your hand now." Again Mrs. Blackwell counts the raised hands, "One, two…

We have our valedictorian. Thank you, staff. Please keep this under wraps and enjoy your weekend. I will make the announcement on Monday at the 2:45p.m. assembly. Teachers, please have your students in the cafeteria by 2:40 p.m."

Mrs. Blackwell commands the attention of everyone as she enters wearing a neon yellow two-piece suit. The color illuminates her coal-black, unblemished skin. Her purple crystal broach is perfectly placed on her lapel. She glides her way to the stage. Moving smoothly, her elongated neck resembles that of a giraffes stride in the bush of Africa.

Her slender hand reaches into her right pocket. She slowly pulls out a pair of cat eye-shaped reading glasses. Placing them effortlessly on the bridge of her nose, she begins.

"Boys, girls, faculty, and staff, it gives me great pleasure to announce this year's valedictorian." Both Keisha and Lavender are on pins and needles. Lavender bites her bottom lip while Keisha, who is sitting on the opposite side of the auditorium, nervously plays with her ponytail.

"I'd like to share a few of the wonderful attributes our nominees possess. Both hold student body offices.

Additionally, each displays good manners, always being very respectful to faculty, staff, and their peers. I am honored to present both students to you today.

Only one will be named valedictorian. Their contributions to ABC have been efficacious. What I mean by that is, they have been useful to staff, classmates, and the community. We are grateful. They are so deserving of this very special recognition.

"Here at ABC, students with the highest GPA are first considered. Next, we consider other factors like behavior, attendance, and extracurricular activities. Consistency is one of the keys to reaching the highest level of excellence. For those of you who are not sure of how to get a 4.0 or higher, an easy formula is to always strive for A's."

A few kids whisper, "I wish Mrs. Blackwell would hurry up." Julietta and Keith are restless. The kids are beginning to shift and squirm as they anxiously await the big announcement of valedictorian.

Mrs. Blackwell talks for what seems like an eternity. "Do you know what the valedictorian does?" Many heads bob up and down in the affirmative.

"Yes, that's right! The valedictorian writes and gives the final speech to his/her graduating class. The valedictorian is someone who is a great communicator, articulates well, commands and captivates an audience."

Now the kids are fidgeting on the floor. Dante and Stina are antsy. They nudge one another. Stina whispers, "She needs to _slow her roll_! I want to know who wins." Teachers and students are rocking back and forth.

So Mrs. Blackwell tells her audience, "Just a few more minutes. I'm wrapping up."

However, she continues with her index finger in the air. "In our society we often think of famous people as being great communicators. Sometimes our admiration  for wealthy people with good looks influences us to admire their speech, even when it's wrong. Many of you know the song titled '_Where you at_?' Although sung beautifully, the singer uses incorrect grammar." Thinking back to just the other day when she used those same words, Keisha cringes. "During an interview, a popular talk show host asked his guest, 'How _was you_ able to do that?' The correct way to ask the question is 'How were you able to do that?" A few teachers yawn. Now Mrs. Blackwell senses she is losing her audience. "A famous rapper makes a poignant plea to 'Stop _lookin'_ at what you _ain't got,_ and start being thankful for what you _do got_.' This powerful message was conveyed using colloquial English. It was most likely done intentionally because the artist preferred to communicate using informal, common, everyday, popular, casual, local, slang dialect for speaking. If the artist chose to get his message across with Standard English the lyrics would be 'Stop looking at what you **don't have**. Start being thankful for what **you have**.' In this case, I think the message would have been as intense if Standard English was used. The point is, it is imperative that every single one of you understand that there is a time and place for colloquial conversation. It's my responsibility, your teachers, and parents to ensure that you know the difference between standard and colloquial English.

The audience applauds. Mrs. Blackwell motions with her hand stretched out in front like a crossing guard motioning traffic to stop! "Thank you, but I'm not finished yet. Please indulge me for just one more minute." Stephanie Singh lets out an audible yawn. Her hand immediately covers her mouth in embarrassment. Continuing, Mrs. Blackwell lectures, "As I was saying, moreover it's up to each of you to learn the difference. It's important to learn appropriate and inappropriate use of language. When you are with your family and friends, you can use your discretion to speak informally."

Keisha feels as if Mrs. Blackwell is speaking directly to her. She reflects on her and Mr. Boyd's conversation. The message is clear to Keisha.

"Sometimes I code switch. Usually my speech is relaxed when I'm not in professional settings. When I'm with my family we enjoy telling stories and jokes. They're usually best when recited using slang. But I wouldn't use informal speech for a job interview, when speaking to my employer, in the general public, or at work. Let me give you another example, when entering my office, I greet my assistant daily saying 'Good Morning', not '*Hey what's up*?' or '*What it do*?'" The entire room breaks out in laughter. Some older students whisper, 'Wow,

Mrs. Blackwell really knows what's up!" Mrs. Sanchez leans over to her colleague noting, "There's no stopping her now."

"Now I'm going to make the announcement you all have patiently waited for. Keisha Wilkerson and Lavender Gray, please join me on stage." The audience erupts in applause watching both girls approach the stage. Keisha has on a pleated blue and green skirt with navy blue knee-high socks and black loafer shoes. Her light blue blouse matches the ribbon around her ponytail. She's wearing her preppy looking outfit today because it's cute, smart looking, and makes her feel like a winner. Lavender is wearing a simple sleeveless purple dress with a ruffled collar. Her purple stud earrings totally match. The blouse underneath her sleeveless dress is lavender, for good luck. Her colors are contrasting well. She's wearing patent leather shiny shoes. Both girls gaze out at the audience with nervous excitement while looking like valedictorians.

Students are whistling and yelling the girls' names. Two girls are whispering. One says, "Keisha got this; she's real cute, smart, popular and always fitted." The other responds, "_Ri-ight_! But she speaks _way more_ slang than Lavender. Have you been listening to Mrs. Blackwell?" Mrs. Blackwell waits for the excitement to die down before continuing. Turning towards the girls she addresses them, "We at ABC School are so proud of you. You both have continuously displayed role model behavior in every category. You are both champions! It was a very close decision, but as I mentioned earlier, only one of you will be this year's valedictorian. Many of your contributions are immeasurable. So in honor of your outstanding citizenship, we'd like to present each of you with a plaque.

"The inscription reads: American Brain Child School honors you for being among our brightest students of the year. Keep doing your best." The audience cheers wildly again. Both Keisha and Lavender are beaming with so much joy their faces radiate the room, like a full moon on a clear dark night. Mrs. Blackwell declares with a raised voice,

"Now it's time for me to announce this year's valedictorian." The room becomes extremely quiet. You'd think you could hear a mouse walk on cotton. Everyone is waiting with bated breath. Mrs. Blackwell says, "I am proud to announce that this year's valedictorian and winner of the one hundred dollar scholarship is none other than Miss Lavender Gray." Lavender is filled with excitement and joy. She is elated! Looking across the room, Mr. Boyd gives two thumbs-ups to Mrs. Sanchez. She graciously nods her head with a smile.

Words of cheer ring out continuously. Lavender holds back her tears as she takes it all in. Keisha is the first to give Lavender a congratulatory hug. Their eyes lock, no words are exchanged. Their spirits mesh. They are best friends. Next, Mrs. Blackwell and Mr. Nickens hug Lavender. The teachers approach the stage to congratulate her.

Keisha silently leaves the stage to join friends as they celebrate Lavender's victory. Mrs. Blackwell returns to the microphone announcing, "Teachers you may dismiss your students now." Keisha waits for Lavender so they can walk home together as usual. While heading home, the girls hold hands so tight it is as if they are Siamese twins. Feeling as though they are being transported by thin air, the girls do not feel the sidewalk beneath their feet. Floating smoothly to their homes, many thoughts from the past weeks race through their minds. This valedictorian experience has been like a volcanic roller coaster ride. Emotions erupted, spilled out and sometimes bubbled over. Their friendship was challenged, stretched, and strengthened. Each girl's character grew. Both girls are grateful for the confidence and courage developed between them. Creativity, love, energy, and humility were transmitted as they shared this experience.

Keisha breaks the blissful silence. Looking deep into Lavender's eyes with a tender but serious expression, she says, "Lav, you really are the best person for valedictorian." Lavender's eyes fill with happy tears. With a resounding voice, Keisha tells Lavender, "*Gurl*, I *can't* wait to hear your speech." Lavender awkwardly responds, "Really, Ke?" Keisha dotingly answers her, "Truly, Lav."

Standard English Glossary

About-face	180-degree turn, change in direction.
Affirms	to declare, assert.
Articulate	communicative, clear, and eloquent.
Campaign	a series of planned activities.
Code switching	use of a language or languages used in a variety of conversations. Relates to social groups.
Competitive	spirited, aggressive.
Efficacious	effective and efficient.
Etymology	the history of a linguistic form (as a word) shown by tracing its development and **relationships**
Flabbergasted	shocked, astounded.
Fruition	realizations, accomplishment.
Illuminating	revealing
Incognito	to avoid notice or special attention.
Mesh	interlock.
Mesmerized	hypnotized
Munificently	generously
Nutritious	wholesome, healthy.

Obituary	a notice of someone's death.
Poignantly	make a relevant point.
Poker-face	an expressionless face
Raspy	hoarse, rough.
Sashay	glide, sway when one walks.
Shrewdly	craftily , cleverly
Smirk	sneer, grin
Spy	a person who secretly watches others
Thoroughfare	a road, street, main road, or highway.
Zest	gusto, enthusiasm, zeal.

Let's chop it up; let's talk about it; Let's rap; let's discuss it...

1. Between the two girls, who was your favorite character? Why?

2. Was one girl smarter than the other? If so, which one? How so?

3. Consequently, _____ wins valedictorian. Was she your choice? Why or Why not?

4. Why do you think Lavender has such a good command of the English language?

5. Does this story remind you of a story you've read before?

6. What might you have done if you were running against Keisha for student council president?

7. What do you consider normal amongst you and your friends?

8. Can you think of additional slang words and give the English interpretation?

Acknowledgments

Your undying acclaim for "Grandma's Brown Cookies" continues to give me inspiration. My undeniable desire to help build self-esteem of readers and hearers of my work is why I write. I am truly blessed to have the love of my family, support of my friends and endorsers. I'd like to give special thanks to Yvetta Franklin for working with me to make my vision for this story a reality. Our collaborative effort has produced a work that is uniquely designed to change lives. Thank you, Yvetta.

Ramona Thomas

I thank God for creativity! I appreciate you, Stephanie, for believing in me. I am grateful to you, Boyd, for encouraging me. "Mama, thank you for allowing Ramona and I to invade your space." I am humbled and honored for this collaboration. Thank you Ramona. Together we have developed a work that will affect our young people today, tomorrow, and in the upcoming years. I value what we are portraying in the characters. It is my intention our work will enlighten and empower the path of our youth.

Yvetta Franklin

A Little bit about Ramona

A proud native Californian, she resides in the San Francisco Bay Area with her loving husband and children. Her Master of Education degree is from Holy Names University. Bachelor of Arts degree in Mass Communication is from California State University at Hayward. She is devoted to filling the malleable minds of our youth with positive thoughts to help build self-esteem. Her first book is "Grandma's Brown Cookies." "The Code Switch" is her second book. Her favorite African American Proverb: Each One Teach One.

A Little bit about Yvetta

A fun elementary school teacher in the city of Hayward, California. She has taught first, second, third, fourth, fifth-graders and adults successfully. She has one adult daughter, Stephanie, whom she loves to pieces. Yvetta was nominated and included in "Who's Who Among American Teachers. She has also been written up in the "California Educator" magazine for flavoring her class with humor. She holds an A.A., B.A. and M.S. from Walden University in Education with a specialization in elementary reading and literacy. Piano and reading are her favorite pastimes.

Both authors are available for select readings,
presentations and book signings.
Contact The Code Switch authors at:
Thecodeswitch@gmail.com
Visit- www.facebook.com/thecodeswitch
Visit-www.amazon.com to give your opinion about our
story

DANOV 5 2018

Made in the USA
Middletown, DE
18 August 2018